IN FOCUS...

AMAZING BUGS

CAMILLA DE LA BÉDOYÈRE

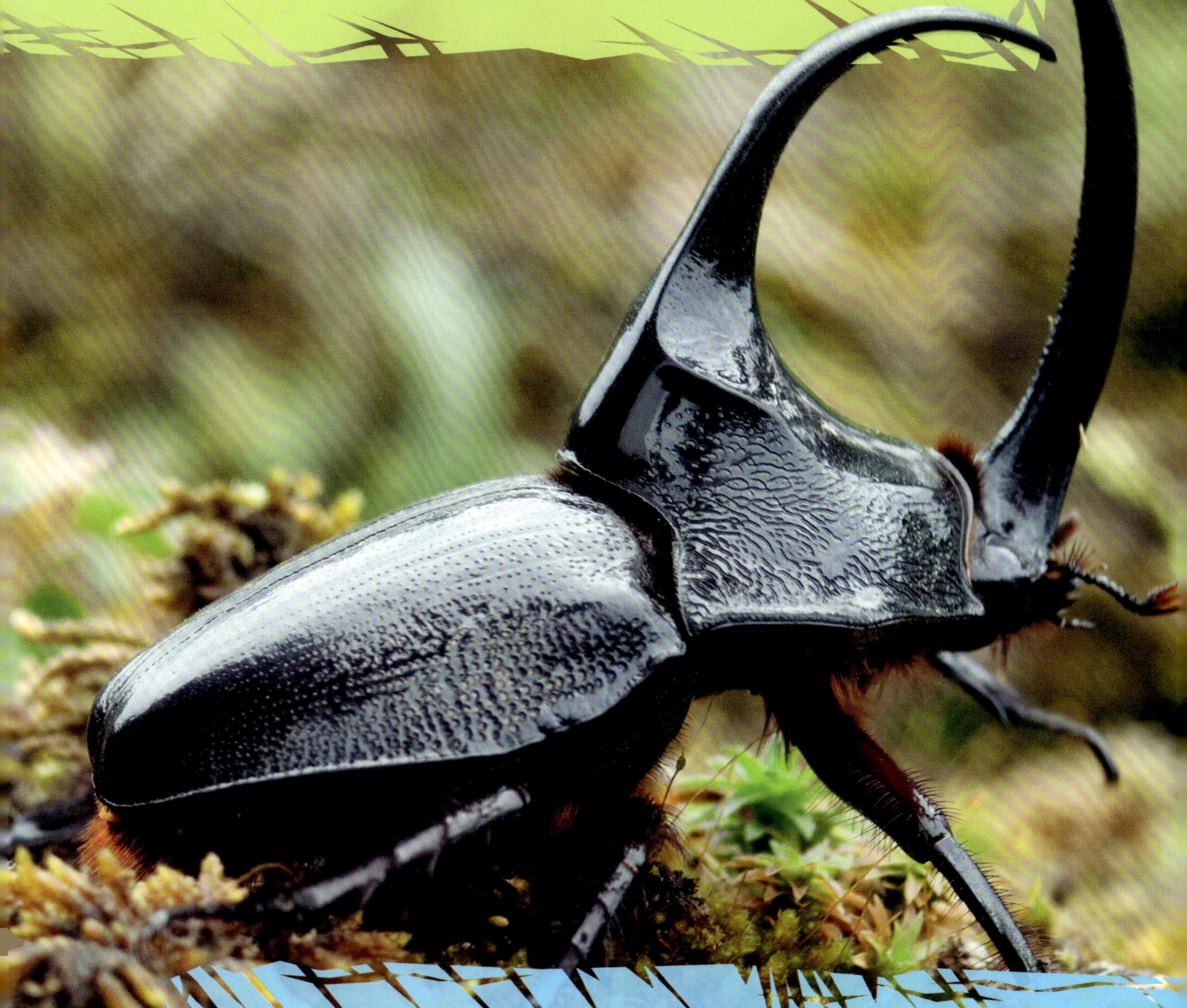

Quarto Library

Quarto is the authority on a wide range of topics.
Quarto educates, entertains and enriches the lives of our readers—enthusiasts and lovers of hands-on living.
www.quartoknows.com

This library edition published in 2019
by Quarto Library,
an imprint of The Quarto Group.
6 Orchard Road
Suite 100
Lake Forest, CA 92630
T: +1 949 380 7510
F: +1 949 380 7575
www.QuartoKnows.com

© 2019 Quarto Publishing plc

All rights reserved. No part of this publication may be reproduced, stored in a retrieval system, or transmitted in any form or by any means, electronic, mechanical, photocopying, recording, or otherwise, without the prior permission of the publisher, nor be otherwise circulated in any form of binding or cover other than that in which it is published and without a similar condition being imposed on the subsequent purchaser.

Distributed in the United States and Canada by
Lerner Publisher Services
241 First Avenue North
Minneapolis, MN 55401 U.S.A.
www.lernerbooks.com

A CIP record for this book is available from the Library of Congress.

ISBN 978 0 7112 4807 6

Manufactured in Guangdong, China CC072019

9 8 7 6 5 4 3 2 1

CONTENTS

*Words in **bold** are explained in the Glossary on page 31*

INTRODUCTION 4
GRASSHOPPERS 6
LONG-HORNED GRASSHOPPERS 8
SHORT-HORNED GRASSHOPPERS 10
MANTIDS 12
LEAF AND STICK INSECTS 14
WATER BUGS 16
STAYING HIDDEN 18
SCARAB BEETLES 20
GLOWING INSECTS 22
RECORD BREAKERS 24
TRAVELING INSECTS 26
BUG WORLD 28
GLOSSARY 31
INDEX 32

INTRODUCTION

The world is swarming with little creatures that have amazing skills for survival. Bugs and **insects** may be small, but they are everywhere. We just have to look carefully to discover a world of super senses, strange life cycles, and speedy hunters.

Wolf spiders carry their young on their backs. This keeps the spiderlings safe while they grow bigger.

Insects use their antennae to touch, taste, smell, and feel. This insect is a glass butterfly.

What is a bug?

Animals without a backbone are called invertebrates. Many of them have tough skin, called an exoskeleton, and they are known as arthropods. There are arthropods in the sea, but the small ones that live on land are the ones we often call "bugs." A "true bug" is a type of insect with sucking mouthparts.

What is an insect?

Insects are arthropods with three body parts and three pairs of legs. Many insects have wings, too. Spiders are not insects because they have two body parts and four pairs of legs. Millipedes and centipedes are not insects because they have many body parts and lots of legs.

FOUL FACT
Millipedes have two pairs of legs on each body segment. Some millipedes have up to 750 legs!

The largest giant millipedes can grow to about 15 inches (38 centimeters) long.

Insect survivors

Insects have survived on Earth for at least 350 million years. They owe their success to their ability to live in many types of **habitat** and eat a wide range of food. There is only one **species** of human, but there are at least a million species of insect alive today.

GRASSHOPPERS

There are more than 11,000 species of grasshopper in the world, and they live in all sorts of places, from tropical jungles to deserts. All types have large heads, big eyes, and strong jaws. Their sight and hearing are excellent, and they are often colored to blend in with their surroundings. Most have two pairs of wings. The narrow front pair is used to cover and protect the back wings. The back wings are wider and fold away under the front wings.

The meadow grasshopper is common in grasslands, moors, and marshes.

A grasshopper's jump is powered by the large muscles in its back legs.

FOUL FACT

Grasshoppers are known for the scratchy, chirping noise that they make by rubbing their front wings and back legs together.

Amazing jumpers

Like all insects, grasshoppers have three pairs of legs. Their back legs are much longer and stronger than the other two pairs. They use their powerful back legs for jumping. Some grasshoppers can travel up to 200 times the length of their own body in a single jump.

Some grasshoppers cover their eggs with a frothy liquid. This mixes with soil and helps to protect the eggs.

Grasshopper life cycle

The female grasshopper lays 15 to 150 eggs in a row, a few inches under ground. The eggs hatch into tiny young, called **nymphs**. As the nymphs grow bigger, they **molt** (shed their skin) five or six times before reaching adult size.

LONG-HORNED GRASSHOPPERS

There are two main groups of grasshoppers—short-horned and long-horned. You can tell the grasshoppers apart because long-horned grasshoppers, such as katydids and crickets, have much longer antennae than their short-horned relatives.

False-leaf katydids can look like fresh, green leaves, dying brown ones, or a mixture of both.

Katydids

Katydids have long, cone-shaped heads and large antennae. Their name comes from the male's song, which sounds like the words "katy-did," or sometimes "katy-didn't." They live all over the world, and can grow to be 3 inches (7.5 centimeters) long. They feed on grass seeds and many of them only come out at night.

Crickets

Crickets are usually green, black, or brown, and have wide bodies, long antennae, and feelers at the end of their **abdomen**. It's said that the snowy tree cricket, or thermometer cricket, can help you tell the temperature (in Fahrenheit)! The trick is to count the number of chirps it makes in 13 seconds, and then add 40.

Crickets "sing" by rubbing their front wings over special rough patches on their back wings.

FOUL FACT
The smallest grasshoppers are pygmy grasshoppers. They measure less than 1 inch (2.5 centimeters) long, and live near ponds or streams.

Katydid disguises

Many grasshoppers protect themselves from enemies by looking like something else. The Brazilian false-leaf katydid looks amazingly like a dead leaf. It hides among fallen leaves on the forest floor and is very hard to spot. Meadow katydids hide in grassy patches and look just like an extra blade of grass!

The colors of this gladiator meadow katydid blend perfectly with the grass stem that it is sitting on.

SHORT-HORNED GRASSHOPPERS

Short-horned grasshoppers have short antennae, usually about half their body length. They include spur-throated grasshoppers and locusts. These grasshoppers are well-known for their rasping calls, which they make by rubbing rough patches on the back wings against the front wings.

Foul Fact

In some parts of the world, people cook and eat locusts as a tasty snack!

Spur-throated grasshoppers feed on grasses, leaves, fruit, flowers, and tree bark.

Spur-throated grasshoppers

These grasshoppers spend most of their lives among grass and other plants. To escape danger, they leap into the air and fly a little way before landing. The sudden flash of bright color on their wings alarms their enemies.

Desert locusts

Locusts are famous for causing serious damage to **crops**. When there is plenty of food around, they live and feed alone. But when food is hard to find, they gather together in huge **swarms** numbering up to 50 billion. The locusts swoop down onto crops and feed until there is nothing left.

Locust swarms, such as this one in Africa, can be carried for hundreds of miles by the wind.

Young locusts change color from green to yellow and black.

MANTIDS

FOUL FACT
Female praying mantids are bigger than males, and they often attack or even eat the male during mating.

Mantids are some of the fiercest **predators** in the insect world. There are about 1,800 species, and most of them live in tropical areas. Their extra-long front legs have large muscles and are much stronger than the back legs. Mantids stretch them out at lightning speed to grab their **prey**, which they hardly ever miss. Mantid mouthparts are also super-strong, and can crunch through even the toughest insect prey.

The legs of the orchid mantis look like flower petals. Camouflage helps them to hide from enemies, as well as prey.

Camouflage

Camouflage is very important for mantids when they're hunting. It helps them stay hidden as they wait for their prey to get close enough to catch. Most mantids are green or brown, so they can easily hide on leaves or twigs. Flower mantids, however, perch on flowers, and are colored to match them.

The praying mantis has sharp spikes on its legs. These help it to hold prey tightly.

Praying mantis

The praying mantis gets its name from its habit of sitting with its front legs folded, so it looks like a person praying. Mantids can turn their heads a long way so they can look back over their shoulders. This allows them to follow the movements of the prey they are about to attack.

LEAF AND STICK INSECTS

Stick and leaf insects look amazingly like twigs and leaves. Their camouflage helps them to stay hidden from predators. There are about 3,000 species. Most of them live in tropical countries, where they eat plants and leaves.

FOUL FACT
The largest stick insect measures an incredible 22.3 inches (56.7 centimeters). Called Chan's Megastick, it lives on the island of Borneo.

During the day, stick insects cling to plants, but at night they move around, feeding on leaves.

Stick insects

With their thin green or brown bodies, stick insects look so like leafless twigs that birds and other predators find it hard to spot them. Some stick insects can change color to match the color of the leaves they are living in. Some stick insects are also known as walking sticks.

Leaf insects

These amazing insects are shaped just like the leaves they live on. They even have similar vein patterns. Their legs are like leaves, too, and their eggs look like the seeds of the plant. As they walk, leaf insects often sway slightly, like leaves in a breeze. Only male leaf insects can fly.

The ragged edges around this leaf insect's body look like the bite marks that you often see on real leaves.

WATER BUGS

More than 2,000 different types of true bug live in ponds, streams, and lakes. Some of them are so light that they can run on the surface of the water without getting wet. Others live and hunt for food underwater, and only come to the surface every so often to breathe.

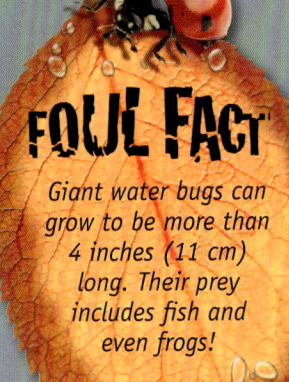

FOUL FACT

Giant water bugs can grow to be more than 4 inches (11 cm) long. Their prey includes fish and even frogs!

Water boatmen use their front legs for eating and collecting food, and the other two pairs for swimming.

Water boatmen

Unlike other water bugs, these soft-bodied insects are not predators. Instead, they feed on tiny plants and algae. Their back legs are shaped like oars and covered in hairs. This helps them to push their way through the water more easily.

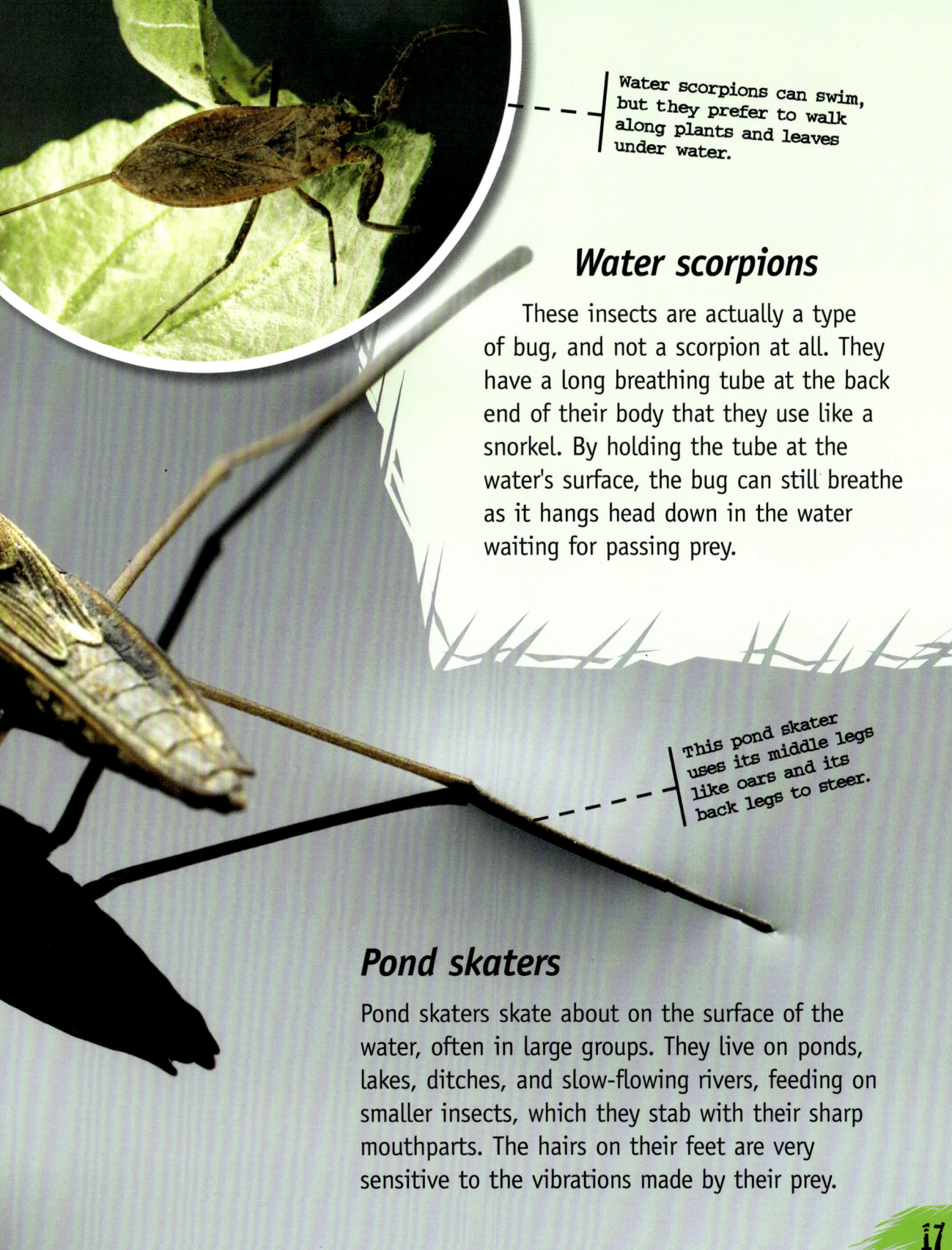

Water scorpions can swim, but they prefer to walk along plants and leaves under water.

Water scorpions

These insects are actually a type of bug, and not a scorpion at all. They have a long breathing tube at the back end of their body that they use like a snorkel. By holding the tube at the water's surface, the bug can still breathe as it hangs head down in the water waiting for passing prey.

This pond skater uses its middle legs like oars and its back legs to steer.

Pond skaters

Pond skaters skate about on the surface of the water, often in large groups. They live on ponds, lakes, ditches, and slow-flowing rivers, feeding on smaller insects, which they stab with their sharp mouthparts. The hairs on their feet are very sensitive to the vibrations made by their prey.

STAYING HIDDEN

FOUL FACT
Some assassin bugs carry a pile of dead ants on their backs. It confuses predators, who leave them alone.

All sorts of animals eat insects, so the insects need to find ways of protecting themselves. For many, the best way is to stay hidden. Some live under stones or leaves, but others are colored or shaped in a way that helps them to blend in with their surroundings. This is called camouflage. It makes the insects hard for other creatures to spot.

With its patchy coloring and straight body, it's hard to tell this geometrid caterpillar from the real twig.

Insect mimics

Some types of insect look just like leaves or twigs, and others are colored like bark or moss. The flower mantis looks like flower petals. As well as helping to camouflage it from predators, this also attracts prey. Its disguise is so good that flower-feeding insects come to investigate. As soon as they get close enough, the mantis catches and eats them.

Orchid mantids are black and orange when they first hatch, but they grow to look like beautiful orchid flowers.

Masters of disguise

Some caterpillars are experts at disguise. The geometrid caterpillar has a pair of grippers at the end of its body that it uses to hold on to a twig. Then it stretches out its body so that it looks just like another twig.

SCARAB BEETLES

The scarab family includes some of the biggest of all beetles, such as the Rhinoceros beetle. Many are very colorful and have unusual antennae that they can spread out to help them sense smells. Some feed on plants, and others eat dung or rotting animals.

FOUL FACT
In just one day, a dung beetle can eat more than its own body weight in animal dung!

A dung beetle's ball of dung can be as large as an apple!

Dung beetles

This group of scarab beetles feeds on animal dung. The beetle rolls a lump of dung into a large ball, buries itself with the ball, and then eats it. Females lay their eggs in the middle of a dung ball, and when the **larvae** hatch, they feed on the dung.

Rhinoceros beetle

This amazing beetle is one of the largest insects in the world. The male's huge horns make up about half its length. It uses them to fight other males over food or to win a **mate**. Females are smaller and have no horns.

Although rhinoceros beetles look very fierce, they are not predators. They only eat rotting plants.

This burying beetle is recycling a dead rat by feeding it to its larvae.

Burying beetles

Burying beetles feed on animals that are already dead. This is an important form of recycling. These flat-bodied beetles crawl underneath a small, dead animal, such as a bird or mouse, and then dig under the body until it sinks into the ground. The female then lays her eggs on the dead body, and later the young beetles feed on the rotting animal.

GLOWING INSECTS

Some insects can glow in the dark. They use special chemicals inside their body to make a natural light. This is used to attract mates, trap prey, or keep attackers away.

Each thread is a trap made by the fungus gnat to catch its prey.

Fungus gnat

Four fungus gnat species in New Zealand and Australia live in caves and other dark, damp places. From their nests, the larvae hang sticky silk threads covered in droplets of glue. When they wave their glowing tail, midges, moths, and other insects are attracted to the light and get caught in the traps. The larvae then pull in their threads and eat their catch.

Fireflies

Fireflies, also known as glowworms, are a type of beetle that can produce a yellowish-green light from the end of their abdomen. Each species of firefly flashes its light in a particular pattern to attract mates of its own kind.

A male Japanese firefly lights up at dusk. Fireflies can make their light brighter or dimmer, and can shut it off.

Foul Fact

Some glowworms use their lights to warn enemies that they taste nasty and should be left alone.

Females of the common glowworm are twice the size of the males and do not have wings.

RECORD BREAKERS

FOUL FACT
Giant beetles can lift about 850 times their own weight, and have jaws strong enough to cut through human skin.

Most insects and spiders are small, but a few grow to be surprisingly big. Some are super speedy, and others have amazing jumping skills. One of the most dangerous is the mosquito, because it carries and spreads **diseases** such as **malaria**.

Giant weta live on islands near New Zealand and are among the heaviest insects in the world.

Biggest and heaviest

The world's longest insect is Chan's Megastick, a tropical stick insect from Borneo. It measures an incredible 22.3 inches (56.7 centimeters) long. The heaviest adult insect is a giant weta, weighing 2.5 ounces (71 grams).

Insect athletes

The tiny spittlebug, or froghopper, can jump 100 times higher than its own length—that's like a person jumping over a skyscraper! The click beetle, for its size, jumps into the air with more power than a space rocket taking off.

Spittlebugs can jump 27.5 inches (70 centimeters) straight up.

The Brazilian wandering spider hunts at night in the jungles of Central and South America.

Danger!

The world's most poisonous spider is the Brazilian wandering spider. Just a tiny amount of its **venom** is enough to kill a mouse. Another very dangerous spider is the Sydney funnel-web spider, which has been known to kill humans.

TRAVELING INSECTS

Many insects spend their whole life on one plant, but a few, such as locusts and butterflies, can fly hundreds of miles. They might travel to escape cold weather, find food, or build a **colony** somewhere new.

Foul Fact
The largest-ever locust swarm contained about 10 billion locusts!

Insect journeys

Some insects make the same journey at the same time each year. This is called **migration**. It isn't only flying insects that migrate. Army ants walk for long distances, and owlet moth caterpillars march in groups to find new feeding places.

Army ants walk for long distances every day to find enough food for their colony.

Locust swarms

When food is hard to find or there isn't enough to go around, young locusts grow longer wings and set off in huge swarms across north Africa and the Middle East, looking for food. There can be millions of locusts in one swarm.

A swarm of locusts may spread over hundreds of square miles.

Monarch migration

One of the longest of all insect migrations is made by the monarch butterfly. These butterflies can't survive the cold winter in northern North America, so they fly south to California and Mexico for the winter. In spring, they return northward and lay their eggs on milkweed plants.

Monarch butterflies (background) gather in huge numbers in Mexico and feed (below) after their long journey.

BUG WORLD

Most bugs and insects live in the warmer parts of the world, especially tropical **rainforests**, where thousands of species can exist on just one giant tree! However, bugs are so adaptable that some manage to live on cold mountaintops, in our homes, or even underwater.

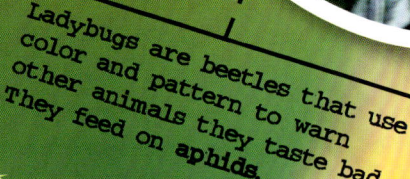

Ladybugs are beetles that use color and pattern to warn other animals they taste bad. They feed on **aphids**.

Perfect bodies

The basic bug body shape may be small, but over millions of years it has changed into many different types. A tough **exoskeleton** gives bugs some strength and support, but it also allows them to use color and pattern to hide. They have jointed legs, which means they are able to move around easily, and some bugs can even use their front limbs to grab and crush prey. Insects are the only invertebrates that can fly.

Identifying bugs

Look carefully at a bug's body and you may be able to figure out which group of arthropods it belongs to. The number of legs, for example, tells you if it is an insect or an arachnid. If an insect has one pair of wings, it belongs to the fly family, but if it has two pairs of wings covered in hairs or scales, it is a butterfly, moth, or caddis fly. Beetles are insects that have hard forewings and chewing mouthparts.

There are over ten times more ants in the world than humans! They usually live in the soil.

Bug Hunt

The best places to look for bugs are in gardens, fields, and parks—anywhere there are plenty of plants for them to feed on. Look carefully at their legs to see how they bend and move. Notice the sensitive antennae on their heads, and think about why the bugs are the color and shape that they are. Always take care around bugs and insects, as some of them bite or sting!

Bumblebees pollinate flowers. Unlike honeybees, they usually live alone.

PICTURE CREDITS

BC = back cover, FC = front cover, b = bottom, c = center, t = top, l = left, r = right.

Alamy: 4tr Matthijs Kuijpers; 4-5 Jerónimo Alba; 9tr Richard Becker; 10-11 frans lemmens; 19tr Thomas Marent/Minden Pictures; 28tr Lukas Jonaitis; 28-29 Antony Cooper; 29tl thatree charoenpornpimongul

FLPA (www.flpa.co.uk) and its associate agencies:
1 Murray Cooper/Minden Pictures; 2 Nigel Cattlin; 6tr Michael Durham/Minden Pictures; 6-7 Alfred Schauhuber/Imagebroker; 7tr Mitsuhiko Imamori/Minden Pictures; 8-9 © Biosphoto, Thierry Montford/Biosphoto; 10l Piotr Naskrecki/Minden Pictures; 11r Nigel Cattlin; 12-13 Bill Coster; 14br Chien Lee/Minden Pictures; 16br Foto Natura Stock; 16-17 Ingo Arndt/Minden Pictures; 17tl Mike Lane; 18-19 Ingo Arndt/Minden Pictures; 20l Mitsuhiko Imamori/Minden Pictures; 20-21 Murray Cooper/Minden Pictures; 21cr Mark Moffett/Minden Pictures; 22cr Michael & Patricia Fogden; 22-23 Robert Canis; 23tl Mitsuhiko Imamori/Minden Pictures; 24-25b Photo Researchers; 24-25 (main) Ingrid Visser/Minden Pictures; 25cr Dave Pressland. 27tr Piotr Naskrecki/Minden Pictures

Getty Images: FC Savushkin

Nature Picture Library: 26br PREMAPHOTOS, 26-27 Sylvain Cordier

Shutterstock.com: BC AgriTech; 5cr suphon phiraksa; 9bl Doug Lemke; 12bl Frank B Yuwono; 14-15 Redchanka; 27b James Laurie; 30 James Laurie

GLOSSARY

abdomen
back end of an insect's body, attached to the thorax

antennae
two long, thin feelers on an insect's head that help the insect to smell, taste, and touch things

aphids
tiny insects that feed by sucking nectar from plants

camouflage
the colors or patterns on an animal's body that help it to blend in with its surroundings

colony
a group of same species insects living together in one place. Ants, termites, and some bee and wasp species live in colonies

crops
plants, such as wheat, grown by farmers for people to eat

disease
an illness that prevents the body from working normally

exoskleleton
the tough outer covering of a spider that protects its body

habitats
the places where animals or plants live

insects
animals with a head, thorax, abdomen, 3 pairs of legs attached to the thorax, and 1 or 2 pairs of wings

larva/larvae
an insect's young, after it has hatched from an egg and before it becomes an adult. A caterpillar is the larva of a butterfly

malaria
a disease carried by mosquitoes that can be deadly to humans

mate
one of a pair of animals that has chosen another to produce young

migration
a journey made by an animal, often at the same time each year, to find food or a mate

molt
to shed, or cast off, a layer of skin ready for a new one to grow

nymphs
the young or larval stage of some insects, such as grasshoppers. Nymphs usually look like the adults, but are smaller and do not have full-size wings

predators
animals that hunt and kill other animals for food

prey
an animal that is hunted and eaten by another animal

rainforests
forests in tropical countries, such as Brazil, that get very heavy rainfall. Rainforests are hotter and wetter than other forests, and are home to huge numbers of insects, other animals, and plants

species
a group of animals with similar characteristics. Animals of the same species can mate and produce young

swarms
large groups of insects, such as locusts, that travel together

thorax
the part of an insect's body between the head and abdomen

venom
a poisonous liquid made by an insect or arachnid to kill prey, or stop it from moving

INDEX

abdomen 9, 23, 31
antennae 8, 9, 10, 20, 29, 31
ants 18, 26, 29
aphids 28, 31
arachnids 29
army ants 26
arthropods 4, 5, 29
assassin bugs 18

bees 29
beetles 20–21, 23, 24, 25, 28, 29
bites and stings 29
body parts 5
Brazilian wandering spiders 25
bugs, true 4, 16–17, 18
bumblebees 29
burying beetles 21
butterflies 26, 27, 29

caddis flies 29
camouflage 6, 8, 9, 12, 14, 15, 18–19, 31
caterpillars 18, 19, 26
centipedes 5
Chan's megasticks 14, 24
click beetles 25
colonies 26, 31
common glowworms 23
crickets 8, 9

diseases 24, 31
dung beetles 20

eggs 7, 15, 20, 21, 27
exoskeletons 4, 28, 31
eyes 6

false-leaf katydids 8, 9
fireflies 23
flies 29
flower mantids 12, 19
froghoppers 25
fungus gnats 22

geometrid caterpillars 18, 19
giant millipedes 5
giant water bugs 16
giant wetas 24
gladiator meadow katydids 9
glowing insects 22–23
glowworms 23
gnats 22
grasshoppers 6–11

habitats 5, 28, 31
horns 21

insects 4, 5, 28, 29, 31
invertebrates 4, 28

Japanese fireflies 23
jaws 6, 24
jumping 6, 7, 24, 25

katydids 8, 9

ladybugs 28
larvae 20, 21, 22, 31
leaf insects 14, 15
locusts 10, 11, 26, 27
long-horned grasshoppers 8–9

malaria 24, 31
mantids 12–13, 19

mate/mating 12, 21, 31
meadow grasshoppers 6
meadow katydids 9
midges 22
migration 26–27, 31
millipedes 5
molt 7, 31
monarch butterflies 27
mosquitoes 24
moths 22, 26, 29
mouthparts 4, 12, 17, 29

nymphs 7, 31

orchid mantids 12, 19
owlet moth caterpillars 26

pollinate 29
pond skaters 17
praying mantids 12, 13
pygmy grasshoppers 9

rainforests 28, 31
recycling 21
rhinoceros beetles 20, 21

scarab beetles 20–21
short-horned grasshoppers 8, 10–11
snowy tree crickets 9
spiders 4, 5, 25
spittlebugs 25
spur-throated grasshoppers 10
stick insects 14, 24
swarms 11, 27, 31
Sydney funnel-web spiders 25

thermometer crickets 9

venom 25, 31

water boatmen 16
water bugs 16–17
water scorpions 17
wings 5, 6, 9, 10, 29
wolf spiders 4